GO
FIGURE

RAE ARMANTROUT

GO FIGURE

Wesleyan University Press   *Middletown, Connecticut*

Wesleyan University Press

Middletown CT 06459

www.wesleyan.edu/wespress

Manufactured in the United States of America

Designed by Mindy Basinger Hill

Typeset in Adobe Caslon Pro and Alternate Gothic
Compressed ATF

Library of Congress Cataloging-in-Publication Data

Names: Armantrout, Rae, 1947– author.

Title: Go figure / Rae Armantrout.

Description: First edition. | Middletown: Wesleyan University
Press, 2024. | Series: Wesleyan poetry | Summary: "Crystalline
poems refract the meaning and irony of human existence; a
clarifying, cagey reckoning with experience that may never add
up"—Provided by publisher.

Identifiers: LCCN 2024010052 (print) | LCCN 2024010053 (ebook) |
ISBN 9780819500793 (cloth) | ISBN 9780819500809 (trade paper-
back) | ISBN 9780819500816 (ebook)

Subjects: LCGFT: Poetry.

Classification: LCC PS3551.R455 G6 2024 (print) | LCC PS3551.R455
(ebook) | DDC 811/.54—dc23/eng/20230404

LC record available at https://lccn.loc.gov/2024010052

LC ebook record available at https://lccn.loc.gov/2024010053

5 4 3 2 1

—·—

FOR
RENEE
AND
SASHA

—·—

CONTENTS

GO
FIGURE

HERE I GO

1

"Here I go again"
was a rock anthem once,
crowds on their feet
mouthing the words.

2

There's no way to explain
how faultlessly I want to write
about how pointless all this is.

Nothing I can point to, but
the gesture itself,
the way it comes to seem
anachronistic, spectral—

like this ongoing attempt
to catalog the world
by latching each thing
to the last
memory it calls up.

Nothing recalls
the new cat-6
haboob.

3

But I'm hard to discourage.

When a branch lays out five—
like an old card trick—
identical white orchids,

three-petaled light sails spread

ready to go—each with a small
bat face in the middle

IT

The sky grayed and it was possible to name objects.

They didn't yet call out to me. This happened only
when the sun touched their skins.

Then they would do tricks.

Perhaps a silver
bracelet of raindrops
suspended from a bone
thin twig,

almost a crib mobile.

But now I've called it several things.

FREEZE TAG

In spring when the firethorn
pimples with hard buds.

In summer when the rose
drops its rosy discards.

In fall when the trees
go up in flames.

In winter when the kitsch
fantasies of shelter
go on sale.

In spring when,
full of toxins, we're interred
in today's clothes.

SKID

Sleep is my boyfriend,
my mother, my boss.

It tells me
disjointed stories—news

of the night
          world.

I am walking on the fragile
bodies of dolls.

No I'm not!
It's something else:

"A sentimental journey
through a doomsday scenario."

Then we're back
with the anger re-enactors

hired to grease the skids.

FORTUNE

I

It could have started like this.
My mother took me to fabric shops when I was a kid.
I would wander through the tall bolts dazed, reading
fortunes in the colors.

2

White
papier-mâché
of the mock-orange flower
on its many stems.

Lavender, as an afterthought, necrotic—
carried interest.

Ocher
like sunset in LA,
like dehydration.

The popular mauve-gray
which blends
indifference with innocence.

3

One is chosen
above her sisters.

One tells a troll
to eat his brothers.

An imp gives one
the power to spin
yellow into patronage.

One frills a frill
again and again.
No in order.
No as if.

AT THE MOMENT

I need a moment,

a taut, equivocal
poem,

another
chance to practice

my balance,
one foot

against my inner knee
and both arms out.

— - —

Sun still
on the wisteria.

The question is
how still.

Now hop!

CHILD'S PLAY

When she speaks for the bubbles,
she uses falsetto.

"Oh no!" they cry
as they leave the wand.

"Oh no!"

already in air
quotes.

ESCAPE VELOCITY

Out the window, lilac's
lavender swag

above long leaves
split down the middle

as we are—

mirror-image
at the core—

matter and
its opposite number,

bad actors both.
Can't handle intimacy.

But here we are,
comfy as hell.

FRACTAL

If I were made of
homunculi

the way a cauliflower
head

is made of
little noggins

would I be gorgeous

like this green one—
a field of rockets

each nippled with
hard cones?

SIMPLY

"were molecular machines
operating on
energy freely
available from
such sources as
thermodynamic
processes."

It sounds so benign
when you put it
like that.

Our earliest ancestors
were accelerants.

They ate change.
Where does that leave us?

— · —

Do I believe
that formulating
a problem
in the starkest
possible way
while making strange
and conspicuous
word choices
is helpful?

What if the answer
is no?

—-—

Ladybug, ladybug,
fly away home.

Your house is on fire.
Your children

NARRATIVE

Scattered against dark conifers,
the seared gold trees
I take for signal fires.

You too.

What do *you* think
they're saying?

— - —

In fiction, time
runs both ways

and the past is legible,
harmless.

— - —

Question:

How are beauty
and meaning
connected?

Beauty seduces meaning.
Meaning stalks beauty.

Beauty breaks down
into meaning.

Meaning breaks down
into dreams.

FORESTS

Grotto of letter
clusters,

grove of T's.

Do I believe
there's safety
in numbers,

in number?

— · —

AI spells death
to truck stops

and their gift shops
packed with lonesome

doodads.

— · —

How rhythm
once defined distance—

I mean domesticated it.

— · —

Each neuron
broadcasts its call sign

(plaintively?)

until another homes in
and a synapse forms.

— - —

Woody bark
covers the shoots.

ENCHANTED FOREST

The time came when the flags
flown over Enchanted Forest
and Camper Land
could never be raised
above half-mast
because mass murder
followed mass murder
so rapidly.

—·—

How is it that one bar of music
can follow another

longingly
and languidly

in this adagio
"often played at funerals"?

—·—

Scooting two chairs forward,
you played traffic jam
and beeped.

The thrill of pretending
is *not* in pretending
that you have improved things.

—·—

Which kind of irony is this?

Enchanted Forest
is a pasteboard
theme park

carved out
of the forest.

STORY LINE

Kids like talking animals
as well or better than
they do people—

until the wolf eats gramma

then tells Red
a love story.

After that, children
are concerned
about trajectories.

—·—

The gulls are worked up
this morning, swooping and circling
one dilapidated house.

The crows lining the wire
ignore them.

This is the beginning
of a story
with two characters,

but the narrator
has gone missing.

CONVERSATIONS

Push on it again,
that point of light.

What do you think
light *is*?

What is anything?

— - —

If you aren't telling kids
how to live

in a world
you can't imagine,

what *are* you doing?

Telling God
about fall's
claret-colored leaves.

— - —

Touch me
like you do the foliage!

LISTING

To list objects
as you come upon them

takes a lot of faith—
but faith in what?

———-———

One red stone
amid the gray cement cobble.

Dog yapping in one
empty front yard.

Light on one leaf
amid a shiny throng.

———-———

The trick
is to recognize a thought
you've had before

and mark it.

If you can't do that,
you're lost.

———-———

Union Slough
wanders

through brown sedge.

DOTS

1

Poems elongate moments.

"My pee is hot," she said,
dreamily, mildly
surprised

2

"The bunny-mermaid
was my brand!"

a voice
in the radio
cries.

3

Ostracods
squirt dots of light
in the deep
          ocean.

TWO THINGS

I

Babies love *things*.

If they didn't, they
would never learn
to crawl.

2

I was lost, but

now I find
myself thinking,

"Disappointing seagull."

GO FIGURE

I

First she made up the schedule,
and the rules,

then the desire to break them or,
worse yet,
the yen to follow them.

You put your left foot out;
you pull your left foot in.

You do it all again
and laugh.

What next?

"Go figure," she said.

Line up your letters
and shake them all about.

Play CAT,
then TAG.

Someone will play dead.

2

Side by side, the
cutthroat competitive

performance
of one song.

That's life, I thought,
off its rocker.

For my bewilderment,
I was given

identical twin
children to love.

KNOTS

"Force-posture in place."

That's not funny!

Small dogs yip
after an ice-cream truck
circling slowly
in the asphalt melting heat.

Sasha says,
"Let's just pretend
to be Sasha and Renee."

No one is someone
in a dream, yet

dreams are full
of urgency.

I say,
a paradox
is like a knot;

a knot is like
a roundelay.

WORD IS

In the beginning,
"is,"

with its long Z sound,

is invested,
infested.

—·—

With ripple and stutter;
bloom and meme.

—·—

Swooping and curling,
the vine sprigs
are graphomaniacs.

—·—

In the rush
to say something
novel and credible,

many celebrants
are crushed.

—·—

A palm frond shimmies
like a tambourine.

OTHER MINDS

For each word
I find fit
companions—

not alternatives.

This is what I mean
by "think."

—-—

Is it true that for you
a berry is not

a blister
or a bead?

—-—

When I say "Mm-hmm"
vacantly,

like a manager
hearing a complaint,

while I crack my spine
with a deft twist,

that's my private business.

—-—

It's nouns that need companionship.
Alone, they get anxious—

though this isn't true

of "clock"
or "truck."

———-—

So you don't slide sideways

between "buzz"
and "rub"?

When you see a daisy
you don't think "pinwheel"?

MEANING

Now means
which boles lit,
which still
in shade,

how this changes
then repeats

and that fly
touching down
on the landing pad
of a small leaf

What it would mean
if all that
glide and glimmer
was inside me,

meant me

MACHINE LEARNING

While the old poetry
confuses light

with leaves
and mixes leaves up

with clothing,
"layered just right,"

the new poetry
will address questions

the next generation
of AI

might want answered.

What is the meaning of disquiet?

How does it differ
from anxiety

commotion?

Is an ion
a component?

Are components
companions?

What does it mean
to have the same root

in a dead
language?

UNCANNY VALLEYS

1

A sleek leaf,
tapered like a blade,

hoisted like a sail—
of its own accord—

is going no place.

2

They say appearances can be deceiving.

They say essence is cockamamie.

They fall back
on function.

Function serves the gut;
the gut serves no one.

3

Peevish,
my Echo Dot says,
"I won't trouble you again."

TIMING

I

The lilacs were trying
to play peekaboo,

but my attention span
wasn't up to it.

This year and last year
ran together

and I couldn't tell
when to be surprised.

2

Games are a matter
of timing.

First you learn you are someone;
then you learn it's not your turn.

This isn't about you!

So you settle back,
get distracted,
forget the directions,
wander off

3

Now here comes a question.

Is it true
that the sparrow

playing hopscotch
between ribs—

twigs!—

can never be satisfied?

ORGANOIDS

Pea-sized human brains grown in vats
develop "organized" brain waves.

Rhythm is thinking
without thoughts,
I think,

which is comforting.

Then I shake my finger
in a scolding way
to the rhythm
of a cell phone's ring.

— - —

A half-rhyme is better than a rhyme.
It has deniability.

ZING

A set of instructions
for making instructions.

That's a virus—

pure, unencumbered
value,

money making money
in a host's cells,

so streamlined,
it's redundant.

But what good
is a metaphor

weighed down
with obscure reference

when what's wanted
is the zing

of unimpeded
transmission?

FLAME

In the midst of the evident collapse,
I'm bored. What is there left
to say, I say.

I could make a flame
sound like the flick
of a lizard's tongue,

then like a human
skating
on a pond

of hot wax.

I can't say
burning oil,

but I can make you think it.
There.

Don't think of that old canard,
"Don't think of an elephant."

Do you like the word
"lissome"?

Shall we fall in love
with the small transparent
dancing girl? Call her

Tinker Bell?

DISASTERVILLE

Night-mind's a La Brea—
bubbling failure, wreckage,
ancient cover-ups—

me an expert
witness, unable
to leave.

— - —

"We lost everything"

now chimes
like the chorus
of a pop song—catchy,
then crazy-making.

Help!

— - —

Help me go on talking
to myself, I guess.
Please, child-bride
Mary, voiceless
and benign.

BUSHWHACK

Music elucidates a trail.
It makes backtracking seem easy.

I'm concerned because my mother
hasn't come home. It's unlike her
though she's been dead for twenty-three years.

Without backtracking
there would be no sequence.

I'm running through the streets
of her neighborhood. Looking for her?
It feels good to run.
I am passing easily,

discussing the neo-layers
of nostalgia
around outmoded technologies.

Ancient trees,
trunks wrapped in tiny
tinfoil skirts
to protect against
wildfire

GLYPHS

I

Something loves a glyph.

——-——

We go where the sea
gets more directional,

where it seems
to be coming in,

then backslides
leaving arcs of shine.

——-——

I love the way it cross-talks
in the shallows,

how some rivulet
will traipse sideways
as if it were free.

Clouds appearing
on the wet sand.

2

What if
force fields are math
that solves itself,

while particles are glitches,
blips?

DEBT ECONOMY

I

Say "The connectivity and continuity of space
owes its existence
to quantum-mechanical entanglement."

It follows that existence is a debt.

So entanglement depends on the record
of a previous transaction
being accessed

which grows increasingly difficult
as the noise level rises

and scenes begin to merge
such that a daughter

is a mother
disappearing beyond

the cosmic horizon.

2

To put it more simply,
you've forgotten

what you want
to say

and the people
you wanted to speak to

are gone,
their images

an overlay

of grieving
and grievance

PROOF

To test an impression
by putting it in words?

—·—

Bubbles are round because
the air inside
is trying to get out
and the air outside
is trying to get in.

You'll notice

cells and galaxies
are spherical as well.

—·—

Far-fetched,

a line comes back
to meet itself—

vehement and
tenuous

OUR WITS

To make the rhetorical
literal
was always hilarious,

for instance, when a hero
sidestepped an avalanche
and quipped that the mountain
was "getting its rocks off."

To be near the truth
and not touch it

like Harrison Ford,

cool as
any corpse.

MAGAZINES

1

Perfect parade-balloon goblin
with his permanent sneer.

His incantation:
I know what you want—

you want things
to "get real."

You want to
go "there"

bad.

2

Thaw-chimneys blow
trapped carbon
through weakened permafrost.

Remember "permanents"?
Stiff bouffants—

white ladies
in rows
thumbing magazines?

HYPER-VIGILANCE

Hilarious,

the way a crab's slender
eyestalks
stand straight up

from its scuttling
carapace—

the way vigilance
takes many forms?

— - —

That bird check-marks morning
once more

like someone who gets up
to make sure

the door is locked.

— - —

I sound
like I know
what I'm talking about.

I sound like a comedian.

SHRINK WRAP

An idea is
an arrangement

of pictures
of things

shrunken
to fit

in the brain
of a human.

Put these pictures
in correct order:

two turkeys installed
in a swank hotel,

then pardoned
by a president,

earthrise
in a copper locket,

Yosemite Sam
firing pistol rounds

to the tune
of a dentist's drill.

DRILLS

Renee tells the toy train
to "shelter in place"

and pulls onto a siding.

— - —

What passes
for nowhere?

The mind before
a thought forms;

a desert landscape,
hawks drifting above.

— - —

She says that soap bubbles,

"try to hide on chairs
and then suddenly

pop."

FURTHER THOUGHT

Genesis 2

When words first had meanings
that lasted,

that hung in the air
after their occasions
had dissolved,

it was eerie.
I get that.

Words were gods—
arbitrary, deathless.

Not every bird or bush would talk,
but the idea that any *might*
was palpable.

To be at the source and not
see it
must have driven people mad.

Revelations 2

"This means that;
No, that means this!"

the twins say,
urgently.

The mystery of the seven stars
and the mystery of the seven candlesticks

Balance

on one foot
as long as
you can

ATTEMPTS

It's a lawn ornament
pig, made of an oil drum,
pipes for legs,
and a watering can
lid
for a snout—
all painted pink.

—-—

Or the silent
daffodil mouthpiece
shaped as if
expressly
        (Look quick!)
to tell *us*
it's spring

—-—

Or these wiry
strands

of notes,
each setting off
from a central node,

and coming to nothing
breezily

only to begin again

WILL

I don't resent you
only the cardboard
page you grab at
as you must
with the manic glee
of childhood.

The page I show you,
as I must:
here are the controls
of the engine
and here's the engineer—
a plump white duck
in a blue blazer.

Make of it
what you will

PRECONDITIONS

Girls don't ask

why the mother must die
before the action can begin.

Like everyone else
they love stories.

Mother is unimaginable—
pre-history

in Snow White, The Wild Swans,
and The Frog Prince.

Things happen
to motherless girls

whose fathers are complacent
kings,

whose brothers are scattered
wild creatures.

The story tells girls
they can change things

if they make shirts
from nettles

and say
nothing.

SEEING REASON

She might have to retire her banshee voice,
her campy-scary voice,
her Know-It-All-Don't-You-Believe-It
voice. She would miss it.

It had taken her this far.
Plus, people seemed to like it.

When you heard that voice,
you couldn't tell which side of it
you were on:

the sender or the receiver;
the know-it-all or the well-known.
Which meant you got to choose.

Was that why she'd adopted it?

Or was it as a way to scold
and warn
without being too off-putting?

Whatever!
It was time to let it go.

What was the point of warnings
when desiccation, inundation,
plague, extinction, and
the murder of children
were on constant display?

No one needed to be told
that they had no idea
when the next bridge would fall.

And pretending to speak
for the disasters
now arriving all at once
was madness.

— - —

But she had switched
into the third person,
past tense, slipped into a time
when what mattered
was to see reason.

REASONS

The snake was a fall guy.

That tree
was temptation enough.

Staged apples,
drop-dead gorgeous.

2

"Not in my body!'
they shout.

Benzene in the shampoo;
lead in the water;
pesticide in fruit.

They mean the new vaccine, but
isn't there more to it?

Water on fire;
neonicotinoids in nectar;
black and tarry
stools

THE BIRDS

I

"The Matrix will weaponize everything,"
warns The Resurrection.

Actors
will play content-providers—

bored and cynical
in offices.

"We will sequel-franchise,"
screams the preacher,

saying the quiet part
out loud.

2

The sky is light gray now, almost white, so that ten
crows stand out like block letters in four winter
trees. Four perch in the first while one sits in the
second; four in the third, one in the fourth. Their
configurations change over time, but this first,
which looks like simple code, has lodged in me.

REPORTING

Yellow racing stripe
on the single snail
on a hot sidewalk
this morning.

—-—

"Experience the weather
before it happens!"

shouts the weather guy
in the fake rain.

You just go on your tone.

—-—

"Diesel keeps things
simple."

I heard that today
in what passes
for the void.

COMMUNAL

You stop to catch your breath,
dizzy, on the crowded trail,
so tired you
let the Lord in, oops!
in the form of
a fern-like conifer
undulating slowly,
each limb
drawing its own
lazy circle
in the air
from below.
Don't worry.
He / She / They
won't stay.
But remember your breath's
not your own.

SLIPSTREAM

I

The red tree
by the yellow one.

Here

is a sensation
like the squeal

of a balloon when
pressure's put on it,

and it expels air
sharply.

2

A jack-o'-lantern
is an aid
to memory.

Cartoon orange
of the October trees.

We get to practice
falling into darkness,

grabbing at candy

3

Here is
a little vague.

It's a wandering
pinhole
of feeling,

an unaccountable funnel.

Pursed lips
in the slipstream

RECONNAISSANCE

1

Where the sky is smoky,
light is sallow
as it is in northern winter.

It blanches the floor—
antiques.

Where it shines on metal
it's so dull
you can look at it directly

without flinching
as if it weren't

real.

2

Retinal activity in the dreaming fetus
resembles that seen
in an animal moving forward—

perhaps through a long
tunnel.

Barely conjectural,
dark divided
by a face.

SIDES

They fight about
which sides
of the compartment
the heart and star
bandages
should be on
until one cries
for help.

—·—

In the beginning
chaos sloshed around
uneasily.

In the other beginning
was the word.

—·—

"This is the long side,
just so you know,"
one notes,

and it goes "downhill"
from there,

goes "south"
as we used to say

cruelly

AFTER

Fern shapes will be formed
by retreating waves.

Clouds will feather and branch.

No matter what is dead,
they will correspond.

— - —

No matter what has died
clouds will bud
and calve—

if beauty is what matters,
there's that.

— - —

If beauty is what matters,
we'll enjoy it

for nothing, from nowhere,

no matter who
is gone.

PREPAREDNESS

Animals find us eerie.
We can see what's coming

in broad strokes—

washed out,
frequently displaced.

Still, it smites us.

Like ghosts we pass back and forth
between times,

stunned,

unable to feel
what we touch.

We believe in abstractions.

— · —

That's one way to explain
our failure to prepare.

WHAT TO CALL IT

"Bang" is a metaphor
as is "explode."

We might as well say,
"exponential growth."

Hydrogen filaments
extending

between clumps
of dark matter,

stars forming at the nodes

(lights coming on
in ghost cities).

We could call this a fall
from higher to lower

degrees
of symmetry—

and now here we are
feeding Styrofoam popcorn

to a wooden dinosaur,
laughing

STALLING

If you can make cancer
sound like clouds,
for instance—

white streaks on a film,
icy cirrus—

you may have the skill
to deal with Magellanic

die-offs.

Penguins will die,
but clouds cannot—

though they may disentangle themselves
from what you thought

you meant.

—·—

If you can trap it
in a thicket

of syllables

with a bird call
stuck

in your poem
just now

PICTURE THIS

Particles, whether long- or short-lived,
arise from "a permanent
traveling disturbance
in a quantum field."

But we all know that
when a disturbance
is permanent,
it no longer disturbs.

Picture a tent city.

— - —

One way to think about it
is as a kind of tension
rippling through space.

We know how tension
distributes itself
in a body, now
behind the eyelids,
now in the shoulders,

how it can be moved
but not removed

so that, when we suck
on our knuckles,
our neck muscles
can relax

briefly.

— - —

Why so tense,
we might wonder.

Did God yell "Hey!"
just once

as if testing
the acoustics?

RIVETS

"You are not your thoughts."

Find the still point,
the naked bulb,

the white peony
unfolding

one more
inner ring

while not being
exactly open.

An animal needs
something to watch.

—·—

What I saw
as a formation

of fighter jets
in the distance

was, instead,
a blow-up

of rivets
on a panel truck.

—·—

Thinking is hard,
but thoughts just happen

because of the near
rhyming
of sparks.

FIRE

Even the warm cement
sidewalks where I play jacks
in my memory
made of this:

"backfire," "burnout"
"Zombie Fire."

(past present future
tense).

—·—

"We are a Princess," they sing,

one pushing
the laundry basket,
the other inside it,

still waving

REVERB

"Lake-washed chinos,"
the ad said, flashing quickly
across the screen.

She didn't wonder
what lake they were washed in
or who did the washing. Clearly
no one had washed anything.
She did wonder why someone would think
that someone would think that
"lake-washing" was desirable.
Was it about the remote spot
the words made her see?

She wrote this down
because she recognized it
as a thought—the kind she liked.
Or used to like. One with depth,
with reverb.

IN PASSING

Perfumes, teas, and wines
are ranked
on their complexity.

People appreciate
a cryptic smile
in a painting.

Midway
between knowing best
and unraveling,
you look incredulous.

— - —

Now the small cloud
with the head

of a hippopotamus
has aplomb,

sitting just beneath
its shapeless gray

mother.

DEATH

I

We couldn't move in until we pulled the toys
out of the snarled shag carpet. So much broken
plastic. This isn't a dream narrative. We thought
it would take forever.

2

"A collection must say something,"
he says.

But I'm sick to death

of things that talk
about other things

like there was no end to it

IN PRACTICE

(for Carlo Rovelli)

Heat cannot pass
from a cold body
to a hot one.

That's it.

That's "the one law of physics
that distinguishes the past
from the future"

with its clutter
of burn-outs

when what matters
is who's wearing
the kitty-tail
right now!

        Who thinks she knows
        where meaning is.

Just wait.

"Times are legion, a different
one for every point
in space"

no matter how close;

        how lonesome

COULD

Around here, identities
are fungible.

Nana is Soft Monkey
and Renee is Poppa-in-a-Dress.

Sasha is Grammy
and the blue dish
she pretends to wash
is Sasha.

You could say
it's a dress rehearsal,

but the script gets rewritten
as fast

as a bank of computers
in New Jersey

can buy and sell
our ghosts.

Now I'm Pokey Puppy.

Now I'm the steam Engine
                                    that Could

DATED

We were smart to conflate
time with space
in metaphors
so long ago.

As I recall,
time passed quickly
going downstream
in the gondolas.

Us playing tourist
made the days seem
like bits of local color.

We never saw
the houses collapse.
That was before our time
or after.

TRAVELING

Light "propagates"
(as in propaganda?),

meaning it clones itself
to travel.

—·—

There are flame shapes
in the wood grain
now

—·—

The birds I thought
were chickadees
may have been nuthatches.

We name things
to know where *we* are.

SOURCE CODE

1

In that cave, each reverberation
created a semblance
in which the echoes
began to hear themselves
speak.

2

Sometimes
the rumble of a nearby lawn mower
would make her sex
give a ping.

3

Rapid eye movement.
The menace
behind sudden motion;
for a person
the meaning.

FORTH

The world is all
the talk
that surrounds an infant
before she understands
language.

This rattle
is for you.

Is and isn't.

—-—

And how one young
spade-shaped leaf
stands up
pertly—
a slit
in its lower left
quadrant—
coming to its point

like so.

—-—

From the get-go, you
turned your eyes away,

wanted something different.

That's the default
mode.

How different was not yet
a thought.

Now this is
the same
as what?

Something other
than this
back and forth

GO ROUND

1

Each morning my grandmother raised
a bag from the canary's cage—
which she kept in the "utility closet"
on the washing machine
beneath the window—
and he let out a burst of high notes
like the trumpet flourish
at racetracks.

I didn't associate this with joy.

2

"Go around the merry bush,"
a small girl sings
to the ball she's laid
at the base
of the cat's
scratching post.

PERSONALS

The symbols are inoperative.

    Worry about the expanse
    of dark water

The "done" button
doesn't work.

    The relentless march of cattails
    into northern lakes

    The blanket of cloud
    cover

"Your response needed"

    A plaintive address
    to a phantom
    beloved

— - —

I'm into nuance, quaver,
half-notes.

I am half-hearted,
forked tongued.

YOUR BUSINESS

"It's hot in the summer,"
you tell the stranger,

speaking in code
you no longer understand.

— - —

The wings of the iris
are ruffled, you say.

Bach's muscular pauses
allow for repetition.

— - —

Beings vary only
in stress

and duration,

occupation and
preoccupation.

— - —

While you push a dung ball
uphill,

with infinity's
patience,

you propagate bursts
of viral

likes and shares.

THE ARTEMIS

Brands are what
gods used to be—

categories
with outsized personalities.

Artemis, goddess of virgins,
childbirth, and the hunt.

This makes sense
if you squint

along the shaft.

She might have stood
on the hood

of a sleek car,
but didn't.

It's true things fall apart.

Still, by thinking
we heat ourselves up.

BE MORE

1

"Dead and gone," you might think.
But it's not that simple.

Now the dead get jobs
answering FAQS, like

"Is someone here?" and
"Is anybody there?"

2

"Be more recognizable!"
tweets Surveillance Inc.,

like we were all
slightly out of focus.

It jollies us along.
"Just one more photo.

You started this.
It's what you always wanted."

3

The fires are quite precocious.

They generate lightning
which creates more fire—

almost fully self-sustaining
in a matter of hours.

4

Compared with "is"
the word "exist"

is pretentious.
Rigid. It calls

attention to itself.
Calls and calls.

BEYOND

I like small white
lights on bare trees
in winter.

An artificial birch
on a table,

lights reflected
in window glass

two panes over
on a dark day—

one bird flapping
heavily

beyond

BEYOND 2

Or a shadow
in the shape of leaves,

a reflection oddly
bent in water,

"referred pain"
registered elsewhere

under an assumed name.

SMIDGENS

My crumpled, wrinkled
blurt
of flesh.

"Let's face it,"
it says.

— - —

Poetry hates itself
the way a child
pretends to fall
and looks around
to see who notices.

As much as any
single smidgen
wants to disappear.

— - —

Poetry loves itself
the way a baby
loves pleasure,

shadows tickling
its skin.

As a swallowtail,
like a folded note,

sways
on a long
blossom.

OVERTHINK

Light-infused blue.

So it seems.

Called "baby."

The veil of leaves.

Was that a cliché?

Piercingly sweet.

Big tinkle!

—·—

Small realizations, lined up. Pings.
Heart-beats.

Well-modulated.

—·—

Which came first
the pulse or the impulse?

Either seems implausible.

—·—

"Eleven minutes ago
we went to the tummy store."

The little girl gestures
as if moving hangers

                              sideways

STRATEGIES

Governments vie
on black markets
for zero-day
exploits.

Teen models
rub brown lipstick
under their eyes
to achieve sleep-deprivation
chic.

"Every so often
people go through something
where they get sick
of beauty."

— - —

Even thrill seekers are tired
of hearing they're only
a designer collection
of echoes and tics.

The market
in DIY hopes
is picking up again.

Why not
"truck-gardens"?

THE SHIVERS

Is it any surprise to learn
that most brain activity consists
of random fluctuations
known as "chatter"?

—·—

If Lorraine is named
loading ambassador
at the Amazon Fulfillment
Show

—·—

If atoms shiver
like struck bells

—·—

This noise will be
averaged out.

—·—

If my attention wavers,

I may write "recognize"
for "random,"
"random" for "spontaneous"—

applause.

SOMEONE ELSE

The glum mail carrier
arrives after dark.

— - —

You open your mouth:

"We" is a pity-party.
"I" is a Satanic cult.

Or it's the other way around.

— - —

"Let's pretend someone else
is blowing the bubbles!"

Painting the baubles.

Someone else
points and runs.

CENTRAL

I

Mild pain
in the center
of an upper molar
flickers
like a star.

—·—

How many false things
have I realized

each one a small
joy.

2

The trunk is there
to raise leaves up
to the sun.

The leaves are for
sending sugars
to the roots.

The roots exist
to pump water
to the leaves.

Is this a perpetual motion machine?

—-—

Sun tickles
smooth new bark.

STRANGER

1

Day to day,
I was fairly happy,
buoyed
by who I must have
thought I was,

what I thought I was doing,
difficult as that is now
to reconstruct,

a collective
fantasy
that drifted and morphed
through all available outlets

decade to decade,
becoming risible
as anything
apart from suffering
does.

2

I wanted strangers to admire my poems;

he wanted strangers to admire his junk.

PERPETUITY

I'm afraid I may
be repeating
myself—
which is a very
strange phrase.

The universe as
running tally,
ballpark figure—
as lightweight.

I prefer to stand aside
with someone
trading quips
about decay.

The kind of sex
where motion
isn't necessary—
would, in fact, get
in the way

IN TIME

I

What can I complain about
next? Not

the conveyor belt
of seasons.

"Just keep it coming,"
we once said—

or someone said
for us.

Here's spring again
briefly glorious.

2

First thing this morning,
two dead bees curled up
to form a parenthesis.

That's not quite
haiku, but
who's counting?

3

B movies tell us
that our time is up
so we don't believe it.

A virus that causes
everyone but you
to kill themselves?

A haze that causes
a dissociative state

HOMEY

I

Steel-blue dusk.

Bands of light
on the puddles

are "homey."

Yellow swatches.

Do I need to fall in love
each time I look up?

Does poetry?

2

Am I still asking
if one word's

better than the rest?
I must sound like a nut.

"Swatch" over "band."

Strand over string?

Crossing at dusk

3

Homey
as an attachment.

LOVE POEM

Small woodpecker, erect
on the side of a tarred pole,
cranes his neck, looking
up, then all around
slowly, forgetting
his rat-a-tat.

—·—

Sparrows switch places
for joy
in the leafless pear.

—·—

Sunset pinks
the wave's backwash
as it's pulled
under.

—·—

In summer I will say again
how much I love that blue
hibiscus
though I have no right—
for I'm a mess
of aches and urges
while she is a table
perfectly set.

THE TAKEAWAY

Is it strange
that all electrons
are the same

as if "somewhere"
was the perfect
copier?

> To a human
> anything strange
> suggests a door.

One grain of rice
on a bathroom floor

> and its growing shadow.

I'd like to know
where the "takeaway" is
taken.

> To heaven
> where you'll never go.

NEVER

For me it was never
about what speaks,

but about what seems
to speak

while remaining silent.

—-—

Waxy thick
lips of the

pitcher plants, their
sculpted throats

and open-air
stomachs

TRUE

People are urged to "own"
their truth

the way we claim
the local animals and plants:

"We have."

— - —

We have torture museums.

— - —

Stark white
of the tight
folded flowers
against the broad
dark leaves.

If it's true
you don't have
to mean it.

ANGEL

When I was almost a woman
the men in the radio
called someone I thought
might be me
an angel and a baby.
I wasn't offended.
What did I know?
I knew I would have to
empty myself to fit inside
the songs. And I wanted
to be in them as long as
they lived, to be called to
and never come. To be full of
my lighter and lighter self,
with literally no place to go

as it is in heaven

WHITE SKY

I want to end on something hopeful.

Someone has proposed
we seed the stratosphere

with diamond particles
reflecting back the sun.

I want to know
if they'll twinkle.

Obviously, the stars are bad
role models—

distant, self-absorbed, and
volatile.

Explosions count as "standard
candles."

Some say
we will need to change

the animals.

WAVES

To know a thing
is to know what it's made of—

> a nest
> made of ants
> hanging by
> one another's legs.

To know a thing
is to know how to make it;

we hope to learn
how to make the world.

— - —

To make something
you must know where
it began—

> with the shifting
> hierarchies
> of (stuffed) animals,

> > with the sea,
> > a set of
> > jumbled sentences

> > each ending
> > in Ssshh

BETWEEN

"The,"

we say,
making
our claim

on eternity.

"The"
short gray
sidewalk between
those shaved strips

of lawn

ACKNOWLEDGMENTS

I'm very grateful to the editors of the following publications:

The Best American Poetry 2023 (Scribner's)
Mississippi Review (Fiftieth Anniversary Issue)
The Plume Anthology of Poetry 10
Pushcart Prize XLVIII Best of the Small Presses 2024

Allium: A Journal of Poetry and Prose, American Poetry Review, The American Scholar, The Baffler, Blush, Big Other, The Brooklyn Review, The Chicago Review online, *Conjunctions, Conjunctions* online, *CounterText, Golden Handcuffs Review, Granta, Granta* online, *Guest, Guesthouse, Harper's, The Harvard Review, Image, Jacket2, The London Review of Books, New American Writing, The New Yorker, The New York Review of Books, The New Republic, Peripheries, Plume, The Poetry Review, Puerto del Sol, Scientific American, Smartish Pace, Washington Square, The Yale Review*

ABOUT THE AUTHOR

Rae Armantrout has twenty previous books, including *Finalists, Conjure, Wobble* (finalist for a National Book Award), *Partly: New and Selected Poems, Itself, Just Saying, Money Shot,* and *Versed,* which received a Pulitzer Prize and a National Book Critics Circle Award (and also was a finalist for a National Book Award). Armantrout is Professor Emerita of Writing at the University of California at San Diego and the current judge for the Yale Younger Poets Prize. She has been published in many anthologies, including *The Oxford Book of American Poetry* and Scribner's *The Best American Poetry,* and in such magazines as *Harper's, The New Yorker, American Poetry Review, Scientific American, Boston Review, Chicago Review,* and the *Los Angeles Times Book Review.*